BEAUTIFUL

DESTINATIONS OF A LIFETIME

PARIS, NEW YORK, SAN FRANCISCO, ROME & MORE

By Livingcolors Publishing

ISBN 9791197931765

FOR THOSE THAT LOVE

TRAVEL, ART, AND EXPLORATION

A FREE GIFT FOR YOU!

Download Art Images for Free!

ENJOYED THE PICTURES?

CONSIDER GETTING THE

FOLLOWING BOOKS

BY THE SAME AUTHOR,

CURRENTLY AVAILABLE

ON AMAZON.COM

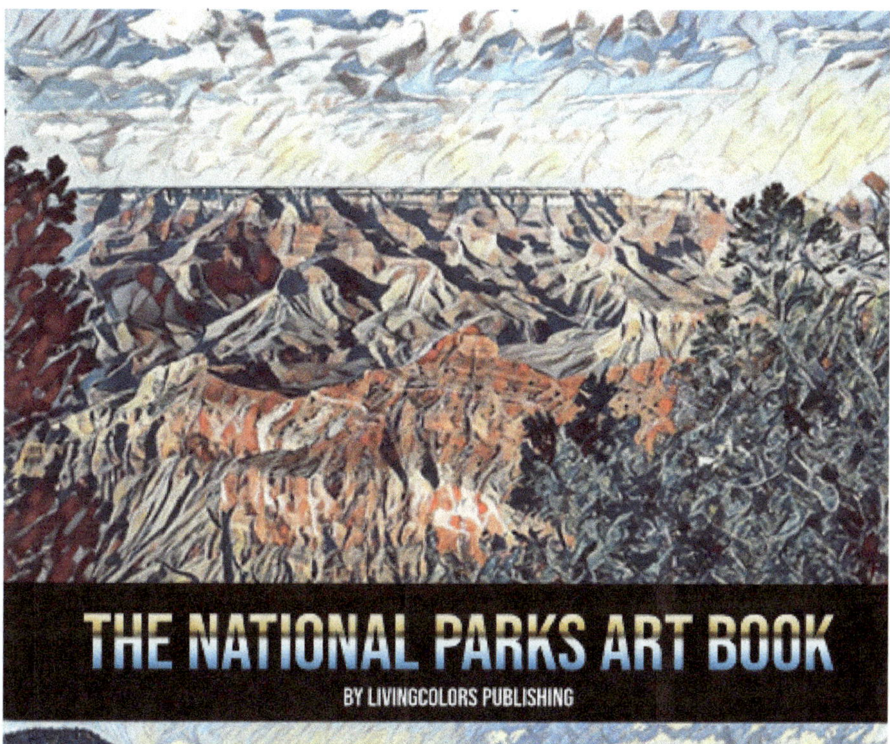

THE NATIONAL PARKS ART BOOK

BY LIVINGCOLORS PUBLISHING

KOREAN CULTURE & KOREAN ART BOOK

LIVINGCOLORS PUBLISHING